EGYPT ABCs

A BOOK ABOUT THE PEOPLE AND PLACES OF EGYPT

Country ABCs

Written by Sarah Heiman ▲ Illustrated by Todd Ouren

Egypt Advisor: Dr. Wagdi Zeid, Cultural Attaché, Egyptian Culture and Education Bureau, Washington, D.C.

Reading Advisor: Lauren A. Liang, M.A., Literacy Education, University of Minnesota, Minneapolis, Minnesota

PICTURE WINDOW BOOKS

Minneapolis, Minnesota

Editor: Peggy Henrikson
Designer: Nathan Gassman
Page production: Picture Window Books
The illustrations in this book were prepared digitally.

Picture Window Books
5115 Excelsior Boulevard
Suite 232
Minneapolis, MN 55416
1-877-845-8392
www.picturewindowbooks.com

Printed in the United States of America.

Library of Congress Cataloging-in-Publication Data
Heiman, Sarah, 1955–
Egypt ABCs : a book about the people and places of Egypt/ written by Sarah Heiman ; illustrated by Todd Ouren.
p. cm. — (Country ABCs)
Includes index.
Summary: An alphabetical exploration of the people, geography, animals, plants, history, and culture of Egypt
ISBN 1-4048-0019-0 (hardcover)
ISBN 1-4048-0351-3 (softcover)
1. Egypt—Description and travel—Juvenile literature. 2. Egypt—Social life and customs—Juvenile literature.
[1. Egypt. 2. Alphabet.] I. Ouren, Todd, ill. II. Title. III. Series.
DT749 .H54 2003
962—dc21
2002005986

Arabic words are in *italics*, except for where they are proper nouns
or they have been accepted into the English language.

Salaam aleikum (Suh-LAHM ah-LAY-kuhm).

"Peace be upon you." That's how people greet each other in Arabic, the language of Egypt, a country in northeastern Africa. Over 69 million people live in Egypt. It ranks 15th in world population.

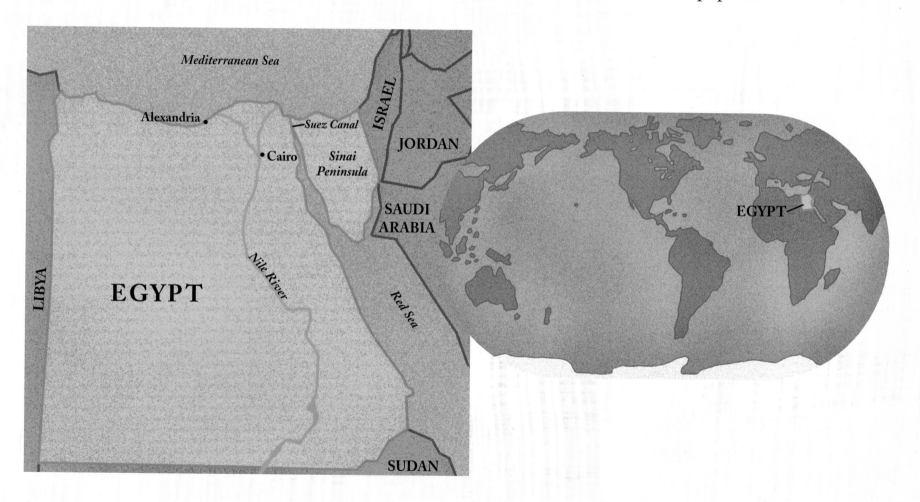

A is for Alexandria.

Aa

Alexandria is a city in northern Egypt, on the Mediterranean Sea. It is Egypt's main port. Founded over 2,000 years ago, Alexandria was once the busiest trading center in the world. Sailboats called feluccas carry goods and people along the water near Alexandria.

B is for backgammon.

Backgammon comes from an ancient Egyptian game called *senet*. Today, playing backgammon is a favorite Egyptian pastime.

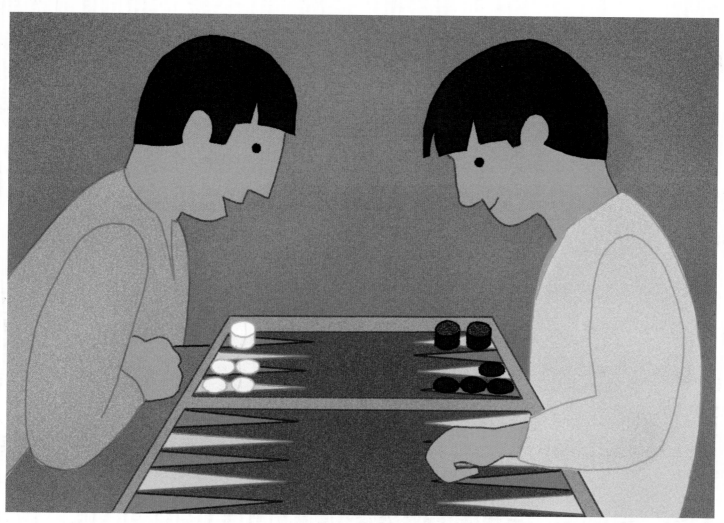

More Fun and Games

Soccer is called football in Egypt. It is the national sport. Horse and camel racing are also popular. Egyptians enjoy water sports such as sailing, scuba diving, and windsurfing.

C is for Cairo (KYE-roh).

Cairo is the biggest city in Africa and the capital of Egypt. Long bridges cross the wide Nile River, which flows through the city. Cairo was founded over 1,000 years ago.

D is for desert.

Egypt is almost all desert. In some places, people travel along wadis—hard, dry riverbeds that wind through rocky hills. Camels have long been used in Egypt to carry people and loads across the sand and through rocky areas. These days, most people travel the desert in jeeps.

People of the Desert

Bedouins traditionally lived in tents and moved from place to place. Some still do, but many have settled down and become farmers.

Berbers live in western Egypt. They have a different language and style of dress than most other Egyptians.

E is for education.

Egyptian children between the ages of six and fourteen are required by law to go to school. A growing number of young people are entering Egyptian universities, which are considered among the very best in the Middle East.

F is for flag.

Egypt's flag has three stripes—red, white, and black. The gold eagle is a symbol of Saladin, who ruled Egypt in the 1100s.

The British government held power in Egypt from the late 1800s until 1952. In 1952, Britain and the Egyptian king were overthrown. Egypt changed its government to a republic. In 1954, Gamal Abdel Nasser became Egypt's first president.

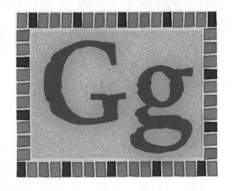

G is for *galabia* (gah-lah-BEE-uh).

Many Egyptian men wear a long, shirt-like robe called a *galabia*. Others wear Western-style business suits or jeans. Egyptian women who follow the Islamic religion wear a head scarf in public that leaves only the face uncovered. Children often mix traditional and modern clothing styles.

H is for hieroglyphics
(hye-ruh-GLIF-iks).

Hieroglyphics is a very old way of writing. It uses picture symbols, or hieroglyphs, for letters or words. Ancient Egyptians used hieroglyphics to keep records and write down their history.

I is for ibex.

An ibex is a mountain goat that lives in Egypt's rocky Sinai Peninsula. Egyptian deserts are home to other interesting animals, too. Gazelles, jackals, scorpions, and many snakes (such as the famous cobra) live in Egyptian deserts.

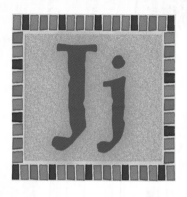

J is for jewelry.

Egyptians take great pride in the many bracelets, rings, and necklaces they wear every day. Egypt is famous for its gold and silver charms (amulets) and name tags (cartouches).

Ancient Symbols Used in Egyptian Jewelry

- ankh: a symbol of life, worn as a good luck charm
- scarab: a beetle that stands for life after death

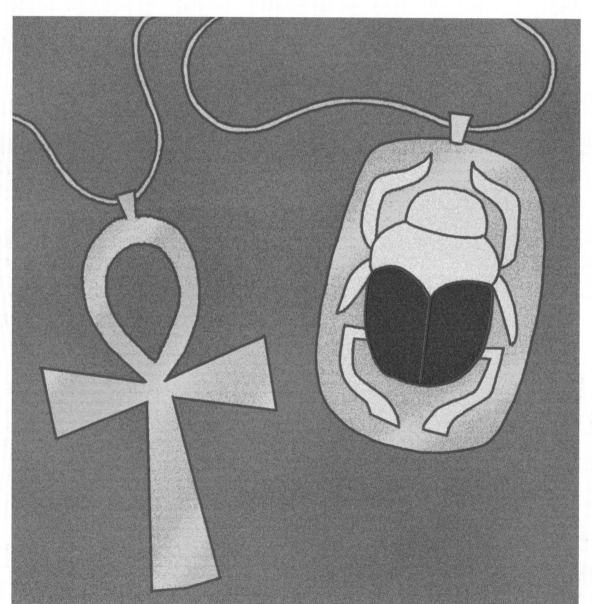

13

K is for Khan el-Khalili
(KAHN el-kah-LEE-lee).

Khan el-Khalili is a famous market in an old part of Cairo. It was built in the 1380s and is a maze of alleys and streets packed with small shops. Smaller marketplaces similar to this are common throughout Egypt. In large cities, people also shop in department stores.

Egyptian Money

The money used in Egypt is called the Egyptian pound. One Egyptian pound is divided into 100 *piastres*, just as the U.S. dollar is divided into 100 cents.

L is for lotus.

Egypt's national flower is the lotus, or water lily. It grows among the reeds along the edges of the Nile River. The lotus image is often used in jewelry, paintings, and carvings.

Papyrus (puh-PYE-ruhss) reeds also grow along the Nile. In ancient times, the stems of papyrus were used to make the world's first paper.

M is for Muslims.

Most Egyptians are Muslims, followers of the Islamic faith. Muslims follow the teachings of the prophet Muhammad. These teachings are found in the holy book of Islam, the *Qur'an* (also known as the *Koran*). Muslims worship in mosques.

N is for Nile River.

Almost all of Egypt's people live near the banks of the Nile. The river provides water for drinking and farming. It also provides fish for eating. The Nile is the longest river in the world.

Many Egyptians earn their living by farming close to the Nile. Cotton is a very important crop for making cloth. Corn, wheat, beans, and fruits are grown for food.

O is for oasis.

An oasis is a green island in the desert. An oasis is formed whenever water bubbles up from deep under the ground, providing moisture for plants to grow.

18

P is for pyramids.

Ancient Egyptians built giant pyramids as burial places for their rulers, called pharaohs. The pyramids were built with huge stone blocks. The most famous pyramids are the Great Pyramids of Giza (GEE-za), just west of Cairo.

The largest of the pyramids was built using about two million stone blocks.

Q is for queens.

Most Egyptian rulers were men, but a few queens also led ancient Egypt. Cleopatra was the most famous queen. She ruled from 51 to 30 B.C. Another queen was Nefertiti, whose name means "the beautiful woman has come." A painted bust of this queen is one of the most famous art pieces in the world.

Queen Nefertiti

Rr

Ramadan is the ninth month of the year in the Muslim calendar. Muslims fast during the entire month, eating and drinking only after sunset. Ramadan ends with a three-day holiday called Eid al-Fitr. Then, people make special meals and exchange gifts. During Ramadan, children light special lanterns called *fanoos*.

S is for Sphinx.

The Great Sphinx stands near the pyramids at Giza. This massive statue has the body of a lion and the head of a pharaoh. The head is six stories high. The Sphinx was built about 4,500 years ago.

T is for Tutankhamen.

King Tutankhamen ruled Egypt around 1340 B.C. He became king when he was about 10 years old and was killed when he was 18. Thousands of items were buried with him, including a gold mask, 415 statues of servants, jewelry, furniture, and 28 pairs of gloves. His tomb was discovered in 1922.

U is for sUn god.

Ancient Egyptians believed in many gods. They thought the sun was the most powerful god—the one who created everything on Earth. The sun god was Ra. Then another god, Amon, also became important. Ra and Amon were combined into one god, Amon-Ra, the King of the Gods.

V is for Valley of the Kings.

Many pharaohs were buried in underground tombs in the Valley of the Kings. In the pharaohs' time, no one was allowed into these secret rooms. Tourists now go there by the thousands.

W is for water.

The water of the Red Sea is not red at all. It is a brilliant turquoise blue. Some people say it got its name from the sea's red coral reefs. Others believe the name came from the red algae that grow in the water.

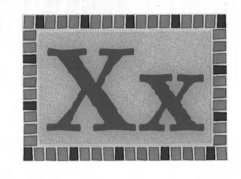

X is for eXports.

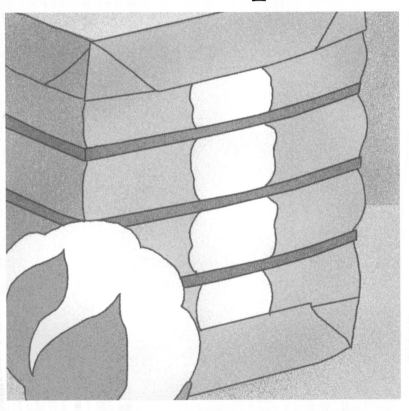

Egyptian cotton and cotton textiles are sold around the world. Other important exports are petroleum (oil) and items made from it. Chemicals and metal products as well as fruits are also exported.

Y is for *a*Y*sh* (EYESH).

Aysh is a round, whole-wheat bread like pita bread. It can be filled with or used to scoop up foods like *ful*, Egypt's national dish. *Ful* is made of fava beans, olive oil, lemon, and garlic.

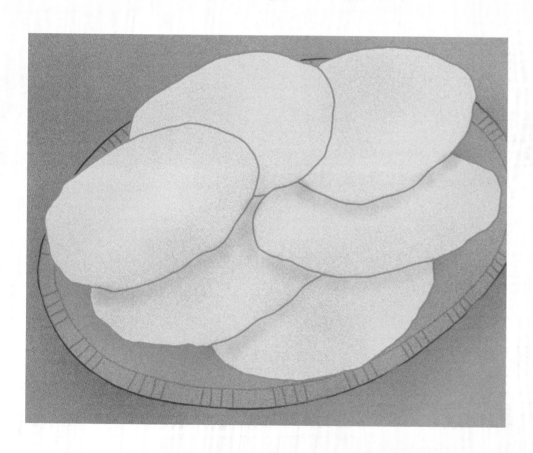

Other Egyptian Foods

- *basboosah*: a sweet cake served with syrup
- falafel: fried balls of ground chickpeas and spices
- *hamam*: baked pigeon
- *kofta*: spicy, grilled ground meat
- *tahina*: sesame-seed paste
- *torshi*: pickled vegetables

Z is for Al-AZhar.

Al-Azhar is a mosque that was built in the year 972. It was named after one of the daughters of the prophet Muhammad. In 975, Al-Azhar became a university as well as a mosque. Classes have been taught there for more than 1,000 years. Today, the university is a major center for the study of the religion of Islam.

Make Your Own Cartouche Necklace

A cartouche is a nameplate or name tag. It is usually in the shape of an oval, and it has hieroglyphs of a person's name written inside the oval. Pharaohs, queens, and other royalty in ancient Egypt wore cartouches. They also had these nameplates carved or painted on buildings. Here is what a cartouche looked like:

You Will Need

- Silver or gold cardboard or sturdy paper
  (or white paper and gold or silver crayons or markers)

- A black marker

- Scissors

- A hole punch

- A ribbon in your choice of color

What to Do

1. Draw an oval about 4 inches (10 centimeters) long and 1½ inches (4 centimeters) wide on the paper.

2. If you are not using gold or silver paper, color your oval gold or silver with markers or crayons.

3. Cut out the oval.

4. Punch a hole about ½ inch (1¼ centimeters) down from the top of the oval.

5. Draw little pictures of things that you like from the top to the bottom of the oval. These pictures will be like hieroglyphs of your name.

6. Cut a piece of ribbon long enough to make a necklace. String one end of the ribbon through the hole, and tie the ends.

7. Wear your cartouche proudly!

Say It in Egyptian Arabic

hello	*marhaba* (MAR-hab-ah)	good-bye	*ma'a s-salama* (MAH-ah sah-LAH-mah)
no	*laa* (LAH)	yes	*aywa* (EYE-wah)

Fast Facts

Official name: Arab Republic of Egypt

Capital: Cairo

Official language: Arabic

Population: 69,536,644

Area: 386,660 square miles (1,001,450 square kilometers)

Highest point: Gebel Katarinah (Mount Catherine), 8,625 feet (2,629 meters)

Lowest point: Qattara Depression, 436 feet (133 meters) below sea level

Type of government: republic

Head of state: president

Head of government: prime minister

Natural resources: petroleum, natural gas, iron ore

Major industries: textiles, food processing, tourism, chemicals

Major agricultural products: cotton, rice, corn, wheat, beans

Chief exports: crude oil and petroleum products, cotton, yarn

National bird: kestral

National flower: water lily

Fun Facts

• Ancient Egyptians developed the science of astronomy and the modern calendar. They studied the
  paths of the stars and planets to predict when the Nile River would flood each year. This helped them
  divide the year into 12 months and 365 days.

• Queen Hatshepsut wanted people to know she was just as important as a pharaoh.
  She even wore the headdress and false beard that pharaohs wore.

• Ancient Egyptians were fond of shaving. A bald head was considered beautiful on a woman.
  Men shaved their heads and faces before they went into battle so their enemies did not have
  as much to grab. People shaved their eyebrows when they were mourning the death of their cat.

• Killing a cat was punishable by death in ancient Egypt.

Glossary

Arabic (AIR-uh-bik)—the main language of Egypt

cartouche (kar-TOOSH)—an oval with a ruler's name inside it; a nameplate or name tag

hieroglyphics (hye-ruh-GLIF-iks)—an early form of writing using picture symbols called hieroglyphs

Islam (ISS-luhm)—a religion founded in the seventh century by Muhammad

mosque (MAHSK)—a Muslim place of worship

Muslim (MUHZ-luhm)—a follower of the religion of Islam.

pharaoh (FAIR-oh)—a male ruler of ancient Egypt

prophet (PROF-it)—a messenger of God, or a person who tells the future

pyramid (PIHR-uh-mid)—a large, ancient Egyptian stone structure used as a tomb for a pharaoh. The pyramid shape has a square base and triangular sides that meet in a point at the top.

To Learn More

At the Library

Cole, Joanna. *Ms. Frizzle's Adventures: Ancient Egypt*. New York: Scholastic Press, 2001.

Deady, Kathleen W. *Egypt*. Mankato, Minn.: Bridgestone Books, 2001.

Marcellino, Fred. *I, Crocodile*. New York: HarperCollins Publishers, 1999.

Osborne, Will. *Mummies and Pyramids*. New York: Random House, 2001.

FactHound

FactHound offers a safe, fun way to find Web sites related to this book. All of the sites on FactHound have been researched by our staff.
http://www.facthound.com

1. Visit the FactHound home page.
2. Enter a search word related to this book, or type in this special code: 1404800190.
3. Click the FETCH IT button.

Your trusty FactHound will fetch the best sites for you!

Index

Africa, 3, 6

Al-Azhar, 28

Alexandria, 3, 4

animals, 7, 12

art, 20

Britain, 9

Cairo, 3, 6, 14, 19, 30

capital. *See* Cairo

cartouche, 13, 29

clothing, 10

education, 8

exports, 26, 30

feluccas, 4

flag, 9

food, 17, 27, 30

games, 5

Giza, 19, 22

government, 9, 30

hieroglyphics, 11, 29

industries

    farming, 17

    tourism, 25

Islam, 10, 16, 21, 28

jewelry, 13

Khan el-Khalili, 14

Koran. *See Qur'an*

language, 3, 29, 30

lotus, 15

maps, 3

market. *See* Khan el-Khalili

Mediterranean Sea, 3, 4

Muhammad, 16, 28

Muslims, 16, 21

Nasser, Gamal Abdel, 9

natural features

    desert, 7, 12

    oasis, 18

    peninsula, 12

    river, 17

Nile River, 3, 6, 15, 17, 30

papyrus, 15

pharaohs, 19, 22, 23, 25, 29

population, 3

pyramids, 19, 22

queens, 20, 29

    Cleopatra, 20

    Nefertiti, 20

Qur'an, 16

Ramadan, 21

Red Sea, 3, 26

religion, 10, 16, 21, 24, 28

Saladin, 9

school, 8

Sinai Peninsula, 3, 12

Sphinx, the Great, 22

sports, 5

Suez Canal, 3

sun god, 24

tombs, 23, 25

Tutankhamen, King, 23

Valley of the Kings, 25